Kryptopithecus gimlinpattersonorum,

A New Species of Bipedal Primate (Primates:

Hominidae) From Humboldt County, California USA

Abstract

Kryptopithecus gimlinpattersonorum sp. nov. is described on the basis of photographic evidence. The validity of the newly recognized biotaxon is discussed and it is concluded that it is not a hypothetical concept.

Key words

Primate, *Anthropoidipes amerborealis*, Bigfoot, *Gigantopithecus blacki*, Hominidae, Sasquatch

Table of Contents

Introduction 1

Diagnosis 3

Description of Holotype 4

    Pelage 4

    Head 4

    Neck 4

    Shoulders/back 4

    Arms/hands 4

    Torso 4

    Hips/Legs 4

    Feet 5

    Holotype Specimen 5

    Holotype Location Data 5

    ZooBank Registration Data 5

Discussion 6

    Evidence Supporting Kryptopithecus gimlinpattersonorum 6

    Evidence Supporting Quality of the Film Footage...................8

    Hypothetical Concept..8

    The Surface Morphology 9

The Gait of Kryptopithecus gimlinpattersonorum......................11

The Anatomy of the Foot...12

Sagittal Crest..13

Achilles Tendon Insertion on the Heel..................................13

Size Measurements..14

Gigantopithecus blacki von Koenigswald.................................14

Similarities of K. gimlinpattersonorum to a Drawing Plagiarized by Patterson..15

Describing New Species Based on Photographs............................15

Conclusion...18

Literature Cited...20

Introduction

"You'll be amazed when I tell you that I'm sure that they exist."

- Jane Goodall (Flatow 2006)

In 1967, Roger Patterson and Robert Gimlin stunned the world with film footage (*Patterson Gimlin Film or PGF*) of what appears to be a large, bipedal, primate walking in a river bed in Bluff Creek, a tributary of the Klamath River, about 25 miles northwest of Orleans, in Humboldt County, California. Termed "Bigfoot", this film provides credible documentation for what was previously considered a mythological creature. In 2007, Meldrum gave it the name *Anthropoidipes amerborealis* ichnosp. nov., on the basis of footprint casts that appear to have been made by the primate in the *Patterson/Gimlin* film.

The *International Commission of Zoological Nomenclature* allows the naming of rare primates to be based on photographic evidence alone (Jones et al. 2005, Li et al. 2015, Mendes et al. 2006). This fact, combined with the fact that Meldrum's name is taxonomically invalid (e.g. see 72.5 & 72.5.1. of ICZN Code of Nomenclature Fourth Edition) led the author to realize that the hominid biotaxon in the PGF can be named as a new species.

Kryptopithecus new genus

Kryptopithecus gimlinpattersonorum new species

Diagnosis: Same for genus and species.

Etymology

Genus: Krypto Greek hidden, Pithecus- Latin Ape.

Species: Named after Robert Gimlin & Roger Patterson who discovered the species.

Diagnosis

Prominent sagittal crest; no forehead; distinct brow ridge; pronounced buttocks; flat feet, with midtarsal break, and fully adducted hallux in line with the rest of the digits.

Description of Holotype

Pelage

Black hair covering body with varying degrees of density; muzzle of face haired; mammae covered in hair.

Head

Prominent sagittal crest; no forehead; distinct brow ridge; nose broad.

Neck

Skull atop slightly curved spine and is positioned below shoulder line; neck relatively short; robust.

Shoulders/back

Broad shoulders and back that appear gorilla-like.

Arms/hands

Powerful arms; hands not elongated; thumbs appear opposable.

Torso

Broad, gorilla-like torso.

Hips/Legs

Tailless; broad hips; well-developed buttocks; powerful legs that appear slightly bent when walking; knees do not appear to lock when walking.

Feet

Feet flat; fully adducted hallux in line with the rest of the digits. Midtarsal break evident (Meldrum 2007).

Size estimates from Glickman (1998).

Height: 7' 3 1/2"; waist perimeter: 81.3"; chest perimeter: 83"; arm length: 43"; leg length: 40".

Holotype Specimen

1967 Patterson-Gimlin film.

Holotype Location Data

A sandbar along Bluff Creek, in Del Norte County, California, midway between Notice Creek and the North Fork. Approximate latitude 123.70 degrees West, longitude 41.44 degrees North (Meldrum 2007).

ZooBank Registration Data

LSID urn:lsid:zoobank.org:pub:3FF8389E-FD2E-4955-A46B-41FC11F18F3C

Discussion

Evidence Supporting *Kryptopithecus gimlinpattersonorum*

The ICZN expressly forbids naming of "hypothetical concepts" and many skeptics consider the Bigfoot a hoax, so some justification of the evidence supporting the validity of the *K. gimlinpattersonorum* as a biotaxon is required.

The strongest evidence supporting the claim that *K. gimlinpattersonorum* is a real animal and not a man in a costume comes from details of the morphology visible in the film.

Consider the following observations indicating extremely life-like anatomy of *K. gimlinpattersonorum* visible in the PGF.

"Mid-Back Drapery Fold: The PGF Hominid has folds inferior to the scapula, consistent with masses of fatty tissue, covered by lax skin folds. It appears consistently on numerous film frames...human surface anatomy...and the surface anatomy of great apes (Pan and Gorilla)" (Munns & Meldrum 2013)

"The Lumbar Fold and Spinal Indentation: The PGF Hominid exhibits the inverted T-shaped indentation, comprising compound curves, over the spinal region (vertical) and at the boundary between the lower back and buttocks (horizontal)" (Munns & Meldrum 2013)

This is also exhibited by humans and Gorillas.

"The Arching Thigh/Buttocks Division (cont'd): Human surface anatomy frequently exhibits a diagonal line or indentation nearly perpendicular to the thigh/buttock division. Also illustrated, are examples of indentations equivalent to the "notch" seen in the PGF Hominid. Such irregularities are quite common in aging human anatomy, with accumulations of subcutaneous adipose tissue." (Munns & Meldrum 2013)

"The Deltopectoral Groove and the Axillary Fold...The PGF Hominid exhibits a characteristic groove that marks the separation of the deltoid muscle and the clavicular head of the Pectoralis Major muscle...human surface anatomy...Surface anatomy of great apes...display equivalent appearance of deltopectoral groove and axillary fold." (Munns & Meldrum 2013)

"The Thigh/Buttocks Subduction. The PGF hominid displays a subduction of the buttock over the thigh...In a human, an equivalent subduction of the buttocks over the thigh can be seen during extension of the hip." (Munns & Meldrum 2013)

"The blotchy character of real hair, which is evident on the Patterson Filmed Subject (PFS) and... the tuff of hair mass on top of the shoulder, and the sudden transition to much less hair mass near the armpit fold and the collarbone region, plus the thinning of hair in the chest region, so we can conclude that the hair patterns of Patterson's Filmed Subject (PFS) do indeed have a credible resemblance to the irregular patterns of real biological subjects (Chimpanzee).*"* (Munns 2009)

"In several places in the Patterson–Gimlin film, groups of muscles in motion can be seen, in the arms, back and legs. One example, is the equivalent of the quadriceps muscle in the human, which is seen expanding while it

absorbs the weight of the subject. Also seen in this sequence, is a structure similar to a knee cap, the shape of which changes like a human knee. This is particularly difficult to forge because of the need for surface conforming material. Surface plasticity in the side torso is seen near frame 352..." (Glickman 1998)

The toes and hands can be seen to flex in several frames of the PGF (Meldrum 2007, pers. obs.).

Evidence Supporting Quality of the Film Footage

"The Patterson-Gimlin film consists of 954 individual image frames... about 40% of them are relatively sharp and do not contain significant motion blur. Of those relatively sharp frames, about 100 may be considered pristine in image sharpness. The film resolution is sufficient to study the details of surface anatomy..." (Munns & Meldrum 2013)

"The camera original was not spliced or edited in any way... Image artifacts can be reliably identified and eliminated... The methods available for altering 16mm film at the time were inadequate for falsifying the image data in any way undetectable to modern technologies." (Munns & Meldrum 2013)

"Thirty-six years have passed and definitive proof of a hoax has not surfaced." (Daegling 2004).

Hypothetical Concept

Given that *K. gimlinpattersonorum* has been recorded on undoctored film, and there is convincing evidence that it is a real animal, it is not "only in the mind of the author" (ICZN [Art. 1.3.1]) and therefore, it is not a hypothetical concept and can be named. This hypothesis may turn out to be false if new evidence is presented, or a new approach to analysis of current evidence is realized; however, this is true any time a new species is proposed and is not unique to this subject.

The Surface Morphology

"The lines, folds and masses on the PGF body, are demonstrated to occur consistently in real human and great ape anatomy through the dynamic interaction of skin and underlying adipose deposits. In contrast, they are consistently shown to fail to occur on fabricated fur costumes employing 1967-era materials." (Munns & Meldrum 2013)

The strongest evidence that supports the hypothesis that *K. gimlinpattersonorum* is a real biotaxon, are the details of the anatomy visible in the PGF. Moving muscles, sagging skin, excess adipose tissue, flexing toes; all details indicating this is a real animal and not a "man in a monkey suit". These anatomical details, visible in the PGF, are strong enough evidence to support the hypothesis that the PGF depicts a real animal, and any challenge to the hypothesis that *K. gimlinpattersonorum* is a valid biotaxon, must falsify these observations of the anatomy.

It is important to note, that these anatomical details are difficult to replicate in a costume today, let alone in 1967. Especially given the materials available at that time (See Munns 2009 especially regarding fake adipose tissue) and this is one of the reasons why modern movie makers no longer rely on full body costumes, and instead use

Computer Generated Images (CGI effects) to create "life-like" primates on film (see Bishop 2017). Here is a quote from the special effects creators of the recent (2017) film "*War for the Planet of the Apes*" to illustrate this point.

"From the beginning… we knew the apes would be completely digital. We didn't look at doing anything with prosthetics, because the whole point of the story was, they had to look realistic, so you would believe it…" (Bishop 2017)

If you want realism, a costume is not the way to go, and in 1967, a costume would have been the only option for a hoax since the CGI technology had not yet been developed. When you look at movies contemporary with the PGF (circa 1968) like, "Planet of the Apes" and "2001 Space Odyssey" the ability to create film realistic, hominid costumes was very limited and they looked phony. In "Planet of the Apes", the costume designers could only make the face look semi-realistic, while the rest of the actors' bodies had to be completely clothed. In "2001 Space Odyssey", the hominids were unclothed, and these were considered the best ape costumes made, up to that point in time, but the costume designers had to use long hair to hide the seams, you can also clearly see that the apes have human proportions, and details such as toe movement and muscle movement are not evident. Also, the transition between haired and hairless parts of the costume were very course and overall looked fake. In summary, these "Hollywood apes", though the best that could be done at the time, lacked the realism and subtle details of anatomy (e.g. body surface morphology, toe flexion, adipose tissue, muscle movement, etc.) that indicate realism, unlike what is seen in the PGF.

It literally took decades for Hollywood costume designers to create a realistic ape costume, and the 1988 movie "Gorillas in the Mist" was the first time a realistic hominid costume was created. There are several important things to realize about this achievement. First, was that the only way to make these gorilla costumes look realistic was to interlace film footage of real gorillas, with the actors in the costumes to create the illusion of realism (Henneman 2015). Second, to create such a realistic costume involved hand-woven hairs and animatronics along with detailed study of great ape anatomy and behavior by costume designer Rick Baker. To get the hair right, it apparently took a team of six wigmakers about five months to hand tie all the hairs into the spandex of the gorilla costume, and it took about 50 sculptors, painters, mold makers, mechanics, puppeteers, suit performers and costumers, etc., to make the apes in the movie look film realistic (Henneman 2015). It is highly unlikely that Patterson and Gimlin had the resources, or access to the resources, to do this, especially since it had never been done before. Also, the scenes in *"Gorillas in the Mist"* with the ape costumes, are relatively brief, and the gorillas are mostly stationary, unlike the individual in the PGF, who is seen walking for a relatively extended period which would expose flaws in a costume.

The Gait of *Kryptopithecus gimlinpattersonorum*

In the past, much has been made about the gait of *K. gimlinpattersonorum* in an attempt to "prove" that it couldn't be a person in a suit and that the animal had a primate-like compliant gait.

It should be noted however, that it is possible for a person to imitate the primate walking gait (Schmitt 2003), so regardless of gait type, what the gait reveals is that a real live individual of hominid was filmed. However, it doesn't solve the issue if it is a previously unknown hominid, or a person pretending to be one.

The Anatomy of the Foot

The foot is clearly visible in the PGF. It is similar to a human foot in that it appears to have a fully adducted hallux in line with the rest of the digits. Unlike a typical human foot, however, it does not possess an arch, is flat and appears to have a midtarsal break like the Chimpanzee and Gorilla (per sobs. See Meldrum (2007). Interestingly, however, flat feet and the midtarsal break are also possessed by some humans.

*"A small percentage of modern humans (*n = 32/398*) possess …a midfoot dorsiflexion characteristic of a midtarsal break. Those humans with a midtarsal break, on average, had a significantly flatter foot than those without."* (DeSilva & Gill 2013)

"The midtarsal break was once treated as a dichotomous, non-overlapping trait, present in the foot of non-human primates and absent in humans. Recent work indicates that there is considerable variation in human midfoot dorsiflexion, with some overlap with the ape foot. These findings have called into question the uniqueness of the human lateral midfoot…" DeSilva et al. (2015)

Given this information, the presence of a midtarsal break in the PGF film footprint casts, cannot be used to unequivocally state that *K.*

gimlinpattersonorum feet are not human-like, and it would take actual study of a specimen to determine more the details of its foot anatomy.

Sagittal Crest

Daegling (2004) claimed that the presence of a sagittal crest of *K. gimlinpattersonorum* in the PGF indicated it was a hoax since he believed female primates don't have a sagittal crest. This is a completely false statement and there are several primate species both extinct and extant whose females have a sagittal crest (Balolia et al. 2017). Most relevant to this point is that in recent studies about 50% of dentally mature female Gorillas surveyed have a sagittal crest (Balolia et al. 2017). The presence of a sagittal crest on the holotype of *K. gimlinpattersonorum* is not atypical, and does not support the hypothesis that the PGF is a hoax.

Achilles Tendon Insertion on the Heel

"There is one frame of the film that, when scrutinized, is also entirely inconsistent with known principles of primate anatomy. Frame 72 shows the film subject from the rear, with the left foot entirely clear of the ground. The subject is at an angle to the camera, such that the viewer can see the foot in profile. The heel is clearly seen to project backward from the shank of the calf, such that rather than taper to the end of the heal, the Achilles tendon appears to insert far forward on the heel…A prosthesis explains what is seen in the film…" (Daegling 2004)

After studying the PGF, it is clear that Daegling's observation is an artifact of the film. In frame 72 the lighting and angle of *K.*

gimlinpattersonorum leg create an illusion of a backward projecting heel. The sun is shining on the back of the leg bleaching it out so that it blends with the background, combined with the odd angle, makes the leg look thinner than it really is giving the heel more prominence. In other frames the heel is clearly not projecting backwards excessively and the Achilles tendon appears normal. Also, if the foot were a prosthetic, the extensive toe movement and foot flexion clearly visible in the film would be extremely difficult, or even impossible, to replicate with 1967 costume technology so this argument against authenticity of the PGF is not supported.

Size Measurements

As noted by Daegling (2004) the actual size and measurements of *K. gimlinpattersonorum* are extremely difficult, if not impossible, to estimate from the film due to numerous variables that cannot be fully accounted for. The author decided to use the estimates of Glickman (1998) with the full understanding that these measurements may be in need of refinement once a specimen is found, or if new methods of measurement from film are realized.

Gigantopithecus blacki von Koenigswald

Grover Krantz hypothesized, that the PGF taxon was *Gigantopithecus blacki*, based on footprint casts of *K. gimlinpattersonorum*, however, no formal taxonomic publication was made to this effect (Regal 2009). Given that *G. blacki* is only known from jawbones, and no bones of *K. gimlinpattersonorum* have been found, his argument for *K.*

gimlinpattersonorum being classified as *G. blacki* is considered inconclusive and not recognized.

Similarities of *K. gimlinpattersonorum* to a Drawing Plagiarized by Patterson

Patterson wrote a book before finding *K. gimlinpattersonorum* called "Do Abominable Snowmen of America Really Exist?" and in this book, he plagiarized illustrations from books and magazines that described previous bigfoot encounters.

Most important to the discussion here is that Patterson redrew an illustration by Morton Kunstler showing a female bigfoot walking through a clearing that is reminiscent to the PGF. It has been claimed by some that this proves the PGF is a hoax.

As (Daegling 2004) correctly points out, however, there are two ways to view this. The first is that Patterson (or someone else) got the idea of making a female bigfoot costume from this illustration. The second is that Patterson saw what others saw namely a female bigfoot. The similarity between the illustrations of Patterson and Kunstler does not support, or falsify, the hypothesis that the PGF depicts a real biotaxon.

Describing New Species Based on Photographs

In the past, new species of primates have been named on the basis of photographic evidence without collection of holotype specimens (Jones et al. 2005, Li et al. 2015, Mendes et al. 2006). This was due to the rare nature of the primates, and the fact they could become extinct if specimens were collected.

Kryptopithecus gimlinpattersonorum, however, is more like an Insect: *Diptera* recently named by Marshall & Evenhuis (2015) in that the type specimen escaped after being photographed and has since eluded capture.

Given the relative uniqueness of this situation, the following quotes from Marshall & Evenhuis (2015) justify the practice of naming a new species solely on the basis of photographs if the type specimen has escaped.

"Article 16.4 of the ICZN Code (ICZN 1999) requires all holotypes that are "extant" to be deposited in a collection, Article 73.1.4 allows for the description of new taxa without preserving a collected specimen by the following statement: "Designation of an illustration of a single specimen as a holotype is to be treated as designation of the specimen illustrated; the fact that the specimen no longer exists, or can be traced, does not of itself invalidate the designation". Additionally, we interpret the wording of Article 16.4 to allow for description of a new species on the basis of a lost or escaped holotype, where the term "extant" means a physically "existing" specimen. Thus, a lost, escaped, or purposefully released specimen is not "extant" ..." (Marshall & Evenhuis 2015)

This exactly describes *K. gimlinpattersonorum*, an escaped holotype that is not extant.

"There are circumstances under which a type cannot be preserved." (Marshall & Evenhuis 2015)

Once again, true for *K. gimlinpattersonorum*. A type has not been preserved because the specimen escaped and the species has never been found again.

"Fortunately, as Minteer et al. (2014) put it, collecting specimens is no longer required to describe a species.... (p. 260)". Collecting specimens is highly desirable, but it is indeed, no longer required." (Marshall & Evenhuis 2015)

The only evidence for *K. gimlinpattersonorum* may be the PGF, and this species may already be extinct. It has to be considered a rare species, and, that it is unlikely additional specimens will be found.

"Even in the absence of a collected type specimen… photography can often provide enough information for a proper description, resulting in a readily recognizable and unequivocally distinct newly named species. The few previous descriptions of extant new species, without a type (or part thereof), have, for the most part, been restricted to large vertebrates, for example, primate species known from only small populations." (Marshall & Evenhuis 2015)

This statement applies to *K. gimlinpattersonorum*.

Conclusion

If it wasn't for the fact that *K. gimlinpattersonorum* is a bipedal hominid-like animal, that has gained a lot of notoriety over the years, this film would be enough evidence to describe it as a new species if it were any other type of primate.

There are many cases where a new species has been described on the basis of a single specimen and in many of these cases the species are so rare that no new specimens were ever found. If the requirement to find multiple specimens to name a species was true, many animals would not have scientific names. While it is ideal to find multiple specimens and to collect a non-photographic holotype specimen, it is not required.

"Science as an institution had its mind made up regarding Bigfoot…What was on the film was of no consequence to that conclusion. The film had to be fake because there was no such thing as Bigfoot." (Daegling 2004)

If we are truly going to take a scientific approach to the bigfoot phenomenon, we have to look at the evidence and make hypotheses based on that. The PGF film provides the strongest evidence for the hypothesis that a large primate (*K. gimlinpattersonorum*) has lived, and may still live, in the Pacific Northwest. Given that no one has been able to falsify this hypothesis, and that there is convincing evidence supporting this hypothesis, it must be assumed, scientifically, that the existence of *K. gimlinpattersonorum* is a valid hypothesis until proven otherwise. That is the way science works. The a priori rejection of the hypothesis supporting *K. gimlinpattersonorum* is unscientific.

It is the author's hope that people reading this paper, will look past extreme skepticism (where the probability to see supporting evidence is zero) and realize that the biotaxonomic standing of *Kryptopithecus gimlinpattersonorum* is a valid taxonomic hypothesis supported by evidence visible in PGF.

Literature Cited

Balolia K.L., K. Soligo, B. Wood 2017. Sagittal Crest Formation in Great Apes and Gibbons. Journal of Anatomy: 230(6):820-832. doi: 10.1111/joa.12609

Bishop B. 2017. How War for the Planet of the Apes turned a visual effect into a reluctant hero: Senior visual effects supervisor Joe Letteri explains the secrets of Caesar — and digital trees. The Verge Jul 18, 2017: https://www.theverge.com/2017/7/18/15988096/war-for-the-planet-of-the-apes-joe-letteri-visual-effects-interview

Daegling D.J. 2004. Bigfoot Exposed: An Anthropologist Examines America's Enduring Legend.

DeSilva J. M. & Gill S.V. 2013. A Midtarsal (Midfoot) Break in the Human Foot. American Journal of Physical Anthropology. DOI: 10.1002/ajpa.22287

DeSilva J.M., R. Bonne-Annee, Z. Swanson, K.M., Gill, M. Sobel, J. Uy and S.V. Gill 2015. Midtarsal Break Variation in Modern Humans: Functional Causes, Skeletal Correlates, and Paleontological Implications. American Journal of Physical Anthropology: 00:00–00.

Flatow I. 2006. 'Sasquatch: Legend Meets Science'. N.P.R.

Glickman J. 1998. Toward a Resolution of the Bigfoot Phenomenon. North American Science Institute.

Henneman K. 2015 The best gorilla puppets and suits that nobody knew they saw. Puppeteers of America. https://www.puppeteers.org/2015/03/16/the-best-gorilla-puppets-and-suits-that-nobody-knew-they-saw/

Jones T., K.L. Ehardt, T.M. Butynski, T.R.B. Davenport, N.E. Mpunga, S.J. Machaga, D.W. De Luca 2005. The Highland Mangabey Lophocebus kipunji: a New Species of African monkey. Science 308: 1161–1164. doi: 10.1126/science.1109191

Li K., K. Zhao, P.F. Fan 2015. White-Cheeked Macaque (*Macaca leucogenys*): A New Macaque Species from Medog, Southeastern Tibet. American Journal of Primatology 77(7): 753–766. doi: 10.1002/ajp.22394

Marshall S.A., N.L. Evenhuis 2015. New Species Without Dead Bodies: A Case for Photo-Based Descriptions, Illustrated by a Striking New Species of Marleyimyia Hesse (Diptera, Bombyliidae) from South Africa. ZooKeys 525: 117-127. https://doi.org/10.3897/zookeys.525.6143

Meldrum J.D. 2007. Ichnotaxonomy of Giant Hominoid Tracks in North America. In Lucas, Spielmann and Lockley, eds: Cenozoic Vertebrate Tracks and Traces. New Mexico Museum of Natural History and Science Bulletin 42.

Mendes Pontes A.R., A. Malta, P.H. Asfora 2006. A New Species of Capuchin Monkey, Genus *Cebus* Erxleben (Cebidae, Primates): Found at the Very Brink of Extinction in the Pernambuco Endemism Centre. Zootaxa 1200: 1–12.

Munns B. 2009. The Authenticity of the Subject Figure Seen in the Film. Release Number 1H: Two Year Review Part Two. The Munn's Report. www.themunnsreport.com

Munns B. & J. Meldrum 2013. Surface Anatomy and Subcutaneous Adipose Tissue Features in the Analysis of the Patterson-Gimlin Film Hominid. The Relict Hominoid Inquiry: 2:1-21.

Regal B. 2009. Entering Dubious Realms: Grover Krantz, Science, and Sasquatch. Annals of Science: 66:1,83-102 DOI: 10.1080/00033790802202421

Schmitt, D. 2003. Insights into the Evolution of Human Bipedalism from Experimental Studies of Humans and Other Primates. The Journal of Experimental Biology: 206, 1437-1448. doi:10.1242/jeb.00279